THE SMART WAY TO BUY A HOUSE!

For First-Time Homebuyers

CINDY FICKLIN
CINDY SAYS, LLC

Copyright © 2024
CINDY FICKLIN
CINDY SAYS, LLC
THE SMART WAY TO BUY A HOUSE!
For First-Time Homebuyers
All rights reserved.

No part of this publication may be reproduced, distributed, or transmitted in any form or by any means, including photocopying, recording, or other electronic or mechanical methods, without the prior written permission of the author, except in the case of brief quotations embodied in critical reviews and certain other non-commercial uses permitted by copyright law.

CINDY FICKLIN
CINDY SAYS, LLC

Printed Worldwide
First Printing 2024
First Edition 2024

ISBN: 9798333319593

TABLE OF CONTENTS

PREFACE 1
CHAPTER 1: Why Buy a House? 3
CHAPTER 2: Choosing a Real Estate Agent 9
CHAPTER 3: Choosing a Good Lender 19
CHAPTER 4: Which House is SMART to Buy? 27
CHAPTER 5: Inspections 42
CHAPTER 6: Off Record Matters 50
CHAPTER 7: Title Commitment 52
CHAPTER 8: Due Diligence Documents and Surveys 58
CHAPTER 9: Appraisals 64
CHAPTER 10: Loans 70
CHAPTER 11: Seller Concessions and Rate Buy-downs 75
CHAPTER 12: A Buyer's market versus A Seller's Market 77
CHAPTER 13: Utilities and Insurance 85
CHAPTER 14: Closing Day 91
CHAPTER 15: Being SMART 95
CHAPTER 16: About Me 101

PREFACE

I wrote this book for anyone who is considering buying a house. It's written directly to first time home buyers, although it's also relevant to **all** home buyers. Some chapters are written when I'm feeling feisty and sassy, and other chapters are written when I'm feeling funny (or at least I think I'm funny). I cried when I wrote the last chapter.

I not only provide to you specific and crucial information that you will need to know from start to finish of your home buying journey, but I also share "Horror Stories" of what can happen if you DON'T know those things.

I give my opinion a lot too, and so I should clarify that not all other real estate agents are going to agree with me on everything I have to say.

So why should you listen to me? Well, at the time of writing this book, I've been selling real estate for the better part of two decades. Last year, I earned International President's Elite, which places me among the Top 1% of real estate agents in the world out of 100,000 agents and 40 countries. And I recently was recognized as "Best of the West."

We can talk more about me later in the last chapter, but let's get started with **YOU** and your home buying journey, and how to buy your first house "the smart way."

Because you can definitely do it all wrong. You can make costly mistakes that will haunt you for years if you're not careful or don't have a good real estate agent helping you through this.

I don't want to terrify you so much that you decide to rent for the rest of your life, missing out on endless equity opportunities. But I do want to give you real world scenarios of when good people have gotten themselves into bad situations simply because they didn't know any better.

Don't worry. You are going to be smarter than that ... because you will have read this book.

CHAPTER 1

Why Buy a House?

If it's okay with you, I'd like to begin with a personal story. Growing up, we moved around a lot, and so my parents were always renters. Every year or two, we moved to a new city or a new state. It was hard to move around so much and have to make new friends, and I was always having to adjust to the next house we rented.

Some of those rent houses were absolutely beautiful, and I didn't want to move. In some of them, we had amazing neighbors, and we were close to all the right places in town so that I could ride my bike to them. Some of them had mountain views to die for and hiking trails right there next to our house. I remember wishing so badly that we could've owned those houses.

But other houses we rented were absolutely disgusting. We always had dogs, and so sometimes we had to take whatever rent-house we could get so that we could have our fur babies. There were times when the carpet was disgusting or the house was cold with terrible heating and cooling systems. One house was backed up to a freeway and was so loud that you couldn't ever relax. Another house had a gross backyard with ticks that killed one of my dogs, and the water was orange.

But when you are a renter, you take what you can get if you love your pets and landlords in the area are constantly advertising "no pets allowed."

Once I reached my teen years, I really wanted to be able to paint my room. Black and white checkered teenage bedrooms with florescent pink, yellow, and green were all the rage back in the 1980's – (*yes, I'm actually THAT old, and I'm as surprised as you are about that.*)

Anyhow, all my popular girlfriends had their rooms painted and decorated that way. But being that we were renters, I couldn't paint any of my walls those colors like I wanted to. So I decorated the best I could with various fabrics, always a little frustrated that I couldn't really make it my own.

Fast forward to the day that I became a first-time home buyer as a young adult, and after Closing Day, I could paint the walls any color I wanted! (*Thankfully I'd grown out of wanting fluorescent-colored walls.*) And I could remodel, plant the flowers I wanted, re-stain the deck, and put in a doggy door for my Siberian Husky at the time.

I bought a house next to a running trail in Denver, and I ran Keno Wolf there everyday. We would run to Stanley Lake, and I would gaze up at the mountains ...

so thankful for the house I was finally able to buy and make my own!

I paid $180,000 for that house, and ended up selling it 3 years later for $240,000. And THAT's when I started to understand that the value of homeownership far exceeds being able to paint your walls whatever color you want. It also grows wealth! (By the way, that house today would be upwards of $650,000!)

Just last week I was showing property to investors who live in my town in Western Colorado. We were looking at homes at the $400K price point.

"Cindy!" they exclaimed. "I remember when these were built 20 years ago, and they were $120,000 brand new. And now they're selling for $400-500K?!"

Yes! Even though we had the Crash of '08 in that same 20-year time frame, many homes have appreciated upwards of $300,000 in just 20 years. Not a bad rate of return on your investment! And even better than that, those home-owners got to use it, live in it, and call it "home" all those years.

Some rented them out, and cash flowed on their investment each month while also experiencing significant appreciation in value.

Of course, there are those years when the real estate market is down, but if you hold onto your investment 3-5 years, generally speaking, you will reap an appreciation benefit that is tough to beat in any other type of investment. (*Not to mention the tax benefit of owning a home.*)

I have some clients who bought a new construction house every 2 years from 2010 to 2022. They also loved to buy new luxury cars, and every time they sold their house, they made enough money to pay off the cars and still have enough down payment to buy the next new construction home. It was extraordinary!

But appreciation values stopped skyrocketing in 2023 once mortgage rates increased. Homes are now appreciating at approximately 1-5% currently in 2024, (and 8% in my town of Grand Junction, Colorado). So although my clients will have to wait longer to experience the appreciation they have enjoyed over the last decade, they are still accumulating positive equity, and they get to live in and enjoy the home as their own.

Let me offer a reality check. Had those same clients only rented over the last 20 years, they would have missed out on $300K of potential appreciation!

I sell real estate all over Colorado. And that appreciation would have been even higher in the resort markets of Vail, Aspen, and Steamboat Springs. I have clients who bought a house from me near Breckenridge back in 2017 for $1.3 million. They sold it in 2021 for more than double that amount!

States like Florida and California have appreciated at extraordinary levels too, while other states have seen more modest appreciation. Still overall, the appreciation of home values over the last 20, 30, 40, and 50 years builds something we call *"generational wealth."*

That is, wealth created from owning property is something you can pass down to your loved ones one day. And it's part of what made this country of ours so special.

If you recall from U.S History, many people immigrated here so that they could own property. Property was either too scarce, too expensive, or in some cases, only the government was allowed to own property.

We don't talk about it enough, but the right to own property in the United States is actually incredibly special. And it's not like God is creating more land. Rather, it is becoming more and more of a scarce commodity. And so the Law of Supply and Demand indicates that one day owning property will become too expensive for the common person here too. It will be something that is only passed down throughout the generations.

Hence, generational wealth.

And **YOU** (*and potentially your heirs*) can be among the wealthy property owners because of the decisions you are making right now.

CHAPTER 2

Choosing a Real Estate Agent

The first step to your homebuyer journey is one of the most important ... choosing your real estate agent. That said, everyone and their dog got a real estate license during the last few years since the Pandemic. After all, it's not really that hard to get a real estate license. But getting a license and actually *knowing* what you're doing to the level of "expert" are two very different things.

So how do you know which real estate agent to choose? Using your 'best friend's sister's aunt' who got her real estate license last month may OR MAY NOT BE the best choice.

Keep in mind that this person is going to make money off of you, and you are going to be dependent on them to be knowledgeable and well skilled in their craft. Giving the job of such importance warrants a job interview and a probationary period, as it does with any job. But many real estate agents will try to get you to sign your life away to them right away.

Other agents are going to get upset with me for saying all this, but as in any job in which someone is working for you, you should be able to employ a trial period to determine if they are going to work hard for you and if they have the professional knowledge needed to best represent you. And if they fall short, then you should be able to fire them.

If you sign a document called a 'Buyer Agency Contract' with them right away, then you are stuck to them for however long the duration of that contract lasts, usually 6 months. And terminating that contract will prove to be very difficult to impossible, depending.

Therefore, I strongly urge you to sign a 'Brokerage Disclosure' specifying that the agent is working initially as just a Transaction Broker. And then later, after you've decided you want to hire them for sure, you can sign a 'Buyer Agency Contract' with them.

- *A Transaction Broker is a neutral third party who facilitates the sale of a real estate transaction.*
- *A Buyer's Agent is someone who works for you and your best interest. In other words, they are your Fiduciary.*
- *A Fiduciary is a trusted source who is obligated by law to act in your favor.*

There is one major caveat to working with a real estate agent who is only acting as a 'Transaction Broker,' and that is that they can ONLY answer basic questions for you. They cannot negotiate for you yet or act as your fiduciary. They cannot pull comps for you to tell you if a certain house is worth the list price, and they cannot serve as the bulldog agent you will want them to be.

That said, as soon as you know this agent is "the one," that's the time for you to sign the Buyer Agency Contract so that the agent can begin working as your trusted fiduciary, or "Buyer's Agent."

So how do you get started in finding that trusted Buyer's Agent?

Ask your friends and family who it is that they trust and why. Get several names and contacts. Text them to discern a time for you to meet with them and interview them.

If they don't text or call you back within a reasonable timeframe, be cautious and maybe don't hire them. This is already a potential red flag that you may have communication issues with them later. (Believe me, there are a number of real estate agents who have communication issues and are unavailable more than they should be.)

Not only will this be a problem for you, but it also means that during the heat of an intense negotiation you could lose out because your agent wasn't readily available.

Once the agent calls you, tell them you are shopping for the right Buyer's Agent, and you'd like to interview them. If the agent refuses to do an interview, think twice about hiring them.

If they say something like, "That's not how this is done," then move on. A good agent who is going to work hard for you will actually be glad to answer your questions. And they will respect why you are asking them.

Here are a set of possible interview questions you can ask:

1) Why did you decide to become a real estate agent? — (Their answer should have something to do with serving people. If it's about serving themselves or their bank account, probably don't hire them.)
2) How long have you been in real estate? — (Experience matters with surgeons, attorneys, and pilots. It also matters with real estate professionals. I realize that everyone needs to start somewhere, but your home is life's largest and most precious investment. I strongly suggest that if you use a new agent, then be sure they have a knowledgeable mentor overseeing all of their work.)
3) What was your ranking in the MLS last year? How many transactions did you close? — (A real estate professional who is really damn good at what they do will be ranked toward the

top tier in the local MLS – "Multiple Listing Service." Of course, there are outliers to this, but as a general rule, I stand behind it.)
4) What awards or recognitions have you earned in your real estate career of which you are proud? — (Someone with the experience and skill that you should require will have a list of awards and recognitions. If they say they don't have any, then maybe think twice about hiring them.)
5) How often are you available to show homes, and if you aren't available, do you have someone else on retainer who can show a house to me? — (This is crucially important. When a new listing hits the market, if your agent cannot show you the house before it goes under contract, then you may have lost your dream home because of their unavailability. This is unacceptable. Every good agent will either be available within 24 hours, or they will have a showing agent on retainer who can get you into the house you want to see.)
6) Tell me about a time in which you failed, and what did you learn from it? — (This question will tell you a lot. If they say they never fail, then they are a liar. If they tell you about a time they cost their client their earnest money, then you probably will want to think twice about

hiring them. (*Side note: We will talk about the purpose of *earnest money* in a later chapter.)
7) Tell me about your favorite real estate transaction. — (If the agent lights up with unbridled enthusiasm in reliving how excited their client was after closing, then this may be your person! If the agent talks about some million deal in which they got paid a lot of commission, you may think twice about hiring them. That is an indicator that they work for the paycheck rather than for the client. And you want someone who is working for YOU first. The commission is just a cherry on top for good agents.)
8) Why should I hire you? — (Again, be sure that they are talking about how they want to serve your needs rather than their own. And they should wow you with this answer. If you detect any red flags, go with your gut on that.)
9) What service organizations do you belong to, or what volunteer work have you done? — (Service minded professionals usually have lots to say in answering this question. Agents who are novice or who are in it to serve themselves usually have very little to share. Think twice about hiring one of those agents.)
10) Can you please provide me with at least three good professional references who I can call. — (Again, this is a job interview. Good real estate

agents have a very long list of past clients who you can call for reference checks. If this question stumps them, then I would think twice about hiring them. Don't just rely on Yelp or Google reviews. Sometimes those are falsified. You will want to be able to ask questions of the reference.)

After you really do your homework, you will feel ready to go forward with the agent of your choice. And it is likely that person will become more than your real estate agent, but also a close lifelong friend. That's how it is for my clients. There is a certain trust there that is extraordinarily special. My clients become family.

HORROR STORY 1:

I received a phone call from someone who had signed a Buyer Agency Contract with a real estate agent who was rarely available. When the perfect property hit the market, they spent over a week trying to get their agent to show it to them. The property went under contract before they could see it, and they were exasperated. They wanted to hire me as their agent instead, but I explained that I could not help them until their Buyer Agency Contract was terminated or expired. And their agent refused to terminate the contract. They were stuck for 6 months with that other agent, who did not represent their needs very well. The house they ended up buying had a myriad of issues, and their agent didn't fight for them to get those ameliorated. They'd already given notice to their landlord, and they had to be out of their rental property by the closing date on the house with all the issues. So they closed on it, and as soon as their agent had her commission, she never called them back. And there they were stuck with a house they didn't want and a long list of expensive repair issues. They called an attorney and realized $400/hour adds up quickly, and they couldn't afford the attorney. They were in a bad place, and the negativity of it exacerbated to other areas of their life. One lost their job and they eventually divorced. Financially traumatic events can do a lot of damage.

Of course, this is only one of the worst examples of something like this happening. But it did happen, and it makes the point that you need to be very careful and mindful of who you hire as your real estate agent.

Case in point, really do your homework before you decide on which agent you are going to hire to represent you in a real estate transaction. Choosing badly could be very costly to you in ways you never imagined.

(If for some reason you decide to choose a novice real estate agent, be sure that person has a knowledgeable and well skilled mentor who is guiding them and supervising them closely.)

LAST MINUTE ADDITION TO THE BOOK: As we were about to go to print on this book, the National Association of Realtors is in the process of settling a lawsuit that could change how the Buyer's Agent is paid. Currently, the Buyer's agent is usually paid by the Seller. But this settlement could force Buyers to pay the commission of their Buyer's Agent. This could be potentially impossible for some first-time homebuyers.

When you sign a Buyer's Agency contract, be sure to HAVE THIS CONVERSATION with your agent. If the Seller isn't going to pay the Buyer Broker fee, then find out who is responsible and how it will be paid. Be sure you feel comfortable and well informed with this in mind. DON'T SIGN ANYTHING that you're not comfortable signing. (If you aren't sure about it, it's a good idea to contact an attorney.)

We are still very much at the beginning stages of this settlement, and the judge still hasn't done his final ruling as of today's writing. But be aware that you need to know what you're signing when you sign the Buyer Agency contract and any Brokerage Disclosure.

CHAPTER 3

Choosing a Good Lender

> **HORROR STORY 2:**

I had some clients who were using a mortgage company that I realized must've been charging them super high fees and points on their loan. They had no idea, but I knew something didn't smell right because of the monthly payment they were being quoted. So I had another lender provide them a quote, and they saved $400/month on their mortgage payment and $1800 in closing fees by switching lenders. It was a good thing I had my hand on the pulse of what a monthly payment should look like at a certain price point. Otherwise, these clients would've spent years overpaying while their loan officer made out like a bandit.

- *Points on loans are fees incurred when borrowing money.*

All lenders are definitely NOT created equal. Some are far from ethical, but they will sure come across as a "great friend" type.

I should mention that I wrote this chapter angry, and I've re-written it in 'nicer language' probably six times. I was a real estate agent during the Crash of '08, and I still have PTSD from what some lenders did that ruined the lives of good people (and it almost took down our entire country).

Maybe one day I'll write a book about what it is was like to be a real estate agent during the Crash of '08. But the good news is that we as a country learned from that, and the likelihood of that ever happening again is pretty small.

- *The Crash of '08 basically happened because lenders were giving mortgage loans to people with poor credit scores and no real ability to pay back the loan.*

But I do still come across lenders who are either shady or ignorant, and they can still do damage to their clients. So it still reasons that you have to be very careful who you hire to do your mortgage loan for you.

Now that I've said all that, please know that there are also lenders who are absolutely amazing and who move mountains for my clients. They are my superheroes in this industry, and I don't know what I would do without them.

(I should mention that when real estate agents say "lender," they are oftentimes referring to the Loan Officer, or "LO." We in the industry tend to intersperse those words with one another. The truth is that the mortgage broker or bank is the real "lender." And the mortgage broker or bank will have an Underwriting Department that will be a huge part of this process, to whom we also refer to as "the lender." It can get confusing, and so I wanted to be sure to explain all that.)

- *Underwriting is the department that determines if you are credit worthy enough and financially sound enough to be able to pay back a mortgage loan.*

Underwriting looks at all your bank statements, tax documents, credit score, and a myriad of other documents that will determine whether or not you qualify for the loan. It can get pretty tedious, and so know that going in. I oftentimes joke that "Underwriting will want your first-born child and maybe the second one too."

Honestly, it feels overwhelming sometimes. But once you get through that process to get a "CTC" (Clear to Close), then you are golden!

After you choose your real estate agent, ask that agent for a list of at least three good lenders. Contact all three of them, and tell them you are looking for the best mortgage rate and lowest fees, but also that you are looking for someone who is an absolute expert in the field who is responsive, knowledgeable, and who will provide you with additional information for first-time homebuyers, *such as giving you this book.*

Keep in mind that these are the people who will be handling your most precious personal and financial information. Your social security number, bank records, investment records, credit card records, etc. You want to be sure they are professional to the hilt! Because there are plenty of shady lenders out there, as evidenced by the Crash of '08.

A good real estate agent will be able to help you with some good solid referrals. In fact, I would expect that they do.

Not only that, but I make it part of my job to be up-to-date on all the BEST and latest loan products out there in the world of lending. I team with a number of loan officers who keep me in-the-know so that I can best serve and advise my clients.

I also make it my job to be on the lookout for potential predatory lending practices so that I can be sure to protect my clients from them. (That said, it's a good idea to beware of some online lenders. That tends to be the area in which we are seeing so many problems today.)

In fact, choosing a local lender is really a best practice, as they have a reputation in town to uphold.

After you've chosen your lender, they will pull your credit. Your credit score will determine the type of loan that you can qualify for. And then you'll start down the process of providing your bank statements, tax returns, pay stubs, and a number of documents that they will need in order to begin the pre-approval process.

Don't let this scare you. It's just paperwork.

Once you find a house that you may want to buy, your real estate agent is going to want to include a copy of your pre-approval lender letter along with the offer. If you haven't gone through the process of at least getting pre-qualified for the loan, then the listing agent of the property you hope to buy likely won't take your offer very seriously.

Listing agents (*real estate agents for the Seller*) need to know that you are not only a 'willing buyer,' but also an 'able buyer,' meaning that you have the means to actually buy the house. And that pre-approval letter is going to be important in that regard.

Lastly, once you are pre-approved, *DO NOT GO OUT AND BUY LARGE TICKET ITEMS!

(*Louder for those in the back!*)

Do not go buy a new car or a camper or even new furniture yet. Depending on your credit score and debt-to-income ratio, that purchase could change everything! Your pre-approval on your loan could switch in the blink of an eye to DENIED!

HORROR STORY 3:

I once had a first-time homebuyer who was pre-approved, and we were passed the inspection and the appraisal processes on the home she was buying. Her lender and I had told her not to buy any big-ticket items, and she said she understood that. One day she asked if we could go take a look at the house she was buying so that she could show it to her parents. We were about 6 days before Closing, and had not received our Clear to Close quite yet. She drove up in a brand new car, and my heart fell into my toes. "Look at what I got today," she exclaimed all proud. "It's okay because I didn't actually buy it. I'm leasing it," she explained. I told her that a lease acts the same as a purchase because it still affects your debt-to-income ratio, and she argued back and said that the salesman at the dealership told her it didn't. I got her lender on the phone right away and he confirmed that in fact the lease operates exactly as a purchase.

Not only would it prevent her from being able to buy her house, but she could likely loose her $2,000 of earnest money also. It was a terrifying moment when she realized she'd been misled by the salesman.

Luckily, she'd made the mistake only a few hours prior, and I knew the dealership owner. I called him and told him of the situation, and they took the car back that day and cancelled the lease paperwork. She got her Clear to Close a couple days later, and became a homeowner the next week. But that situation is one I'll never forget.

CHAPTER 4

Which House is SMART to Buy?

Now that you've gotten your lender and your pre-approval letter, it's time to go shopping for a house! This is the fun part!

Enjoy every minute! Try not to let yourself get discouraged by the houses that are all wrong. Laugh and move on. And then really allow yourself to take in the moments when you think you may have found "the one!"

The home buying process can either be super stressful or really enjoyable. A great deal of that depends on your perspective in how you approach it. So go in with the mindset that you are going to have fun with it!

But which house is the right one to buy?

This is a crucial question! .... First and foremost, can you see yourself living there? Can you see you and your family and friends making joyful memories there? Does it feel like home?

These are important questions to answer. But as a real estate agent, I see the other side of things once my clients go to sell the house one day. They are going to want to make as much money as they can once they get to the point in their lives that they decide it's time to upgrade to a larger or different house.

With that in mind, I always begin with the end in mind ... heavily focused on resale value.

"Resale Value" is key. That is, you are going to want to buy a house that many other people would want for themselves. That way, one day when YOU go to sell it one day, it will sell for top dollar no matter if you are selling in a down market or an up market.

In other words, even though you are the Buyer right now, one day you will be the Seller. So resale characteristics should be part of your decision-making process in which house to choose.

With that in mind, here are a list of property characteristics that are potentially UN-desirable in the resale market. (I didn't put these in any particular order, as they are all relevant):

1) Backed up to or next to a busy road or highway. The traffic noise is a significant deterrent for buyers in a resale market.
2) Low ceilings. Some older homes have low ceilings, and in today's world when 18-foot vaulted ceilings are all the rage, the low ceilings could hurt resale value.
3) Messy neighbors. There really is nothing you can do about messy neighbors, and no matter how well your property will show during

resale, it won't matter if the neighbors are gross.

4) Barking dog. If there is an incessant barking dog next door, people worry if they will ever have a moment's peace.

5) Overzealous Homeowner's Association. If an HOA has the reputation for fining homeowners for every little thing, then you have yourself an overzealous HOA. Not only can this cause challenges to you while you own the home, but it can potentially cause you problems when you go to sell the home later. Overzealous HOA's are a growing issue right now in the United States because it limits the homeowner's right to enjoyment. Be sure your HOA is a reasonable one that keeps the properties in the neighborhood looking good, but won't drive you crazy. We will discuss HOA's more in a later chapter.

6) Expensive HOA's. Some condo complexes have terrible budgeting and accounting methods, and charge exorbitant fees monthly. This could prevent the condo from appreciating at the value it otherwise would have because buyers in the resale market will need to account for the extra HOA cost in addition to their monthly mortgage payment.

7) No Master Bath. — (The new politically correct term for master bedroom is "primary

bedroom." So I should really call it a "primary bath."). Regardless, if the primary bedroom does not have a designated primary bathroom, then it can be harder to sell in the resale market. Bi-level floor plans of the 1970's and 1980's oftentimes have this issue. But sometimes these floorplans are the least expensive and may be okay for you as a first-time homebuyer.

8) One bathroom. — Many "starter homes" have one bathroom, and that's okay. It is better to get into the housing market at the price you can afford. But when you go to sell the house, just know that there will be some feedback that 'one bathroom isn't enough.' It's true that one bathroom can present challenges, but a mortgage payment you cannot afford isn't good either. Sometimes it's a tradeoff. The best scenario is if you can find a way to add a second bathroom to a property. That "sweat equity" will pay off in dividends if you can manage to do it on a strict budget.

- *Sweat equity is the additional potential equity you can accrue if you put your own hard work into updating and improving a piece of real estate.*

9) Small galley kitchen. — These days when you entertain, 'everyone ends up in the kitchen.' And so your kitchen is really a focal point in the

home. A spacious open kitchen with a center island and/or breakfast bar is best for this. But if your kitchen is a small galley kitchen, it will make entertaining harder. And this will be a deterrent in the resale market. You can rip out walls and try to remodel the kitchen, but keep in mind that the kitchen is one of the most expensive areas of the home for which to remodel. It just depends on how low of a price you can contract the home, and how much available cash you have on hand for remodeling jobs.

10) Small primary bedroom closet. — I've seen million-dollar homes sit on the market a much longer time than usual JUST because the primary bedroom closet was too small. In America especially, ample storage space is becoming increasingly more important.

11) Small living room. — A small living room means that the giant screen tv isn't going to fit. You'd be surprised how important this is to the majority of home buyers. A small living room makes resale much tougher.

12) Small backyard. — Backyards are getting smaller and smaller in new construction homes. That's because land is becoming more and more scarce. Smaller backyards don't sell as well as bigger ones, and it could impact the price once you go to sell the house. On the other

hand, some people like the lock-n-leave potential of a smaller backyard.
13) Outdated. — When a property is outdated, the resale value is lower. And if you are trying to sell in a Buyer's Market (in which there are lots of homes on the market), if your house is dated, then you will have to it sell at a much lower price, or else make the investment to update the property on a budget.
14) Stigmatized property. — Depending on the state in which you live, the Seller of a property may or may not have to disclose if a murder or death occurred on the property. In Texas, you are required to disclose it. In Colorado, you are actually encouraged not to disclose it. Either way, if the property is stigmatized, it could be very difficult to sell in a resale market.

- *Stigmatized property is property in which a death, murder, rape, or other traumatic event occurred.*

15) LOCATION, LOCATION, LOCATION!! — I purposefully saved the best for last. If you buy a property in a poor location known for lots of crime, registered sex offenders living nearby, or an area known to be "depressed," then your resale value will likely be affected. For investment purposes, it is usually better to buy less of a house in a highly sought-after location than a nicer house in a depressed location. Of

course, there are outliers. Some depressed areas receive a stimulus from government or developers such that it "brings up the area." In that case, it's actually potentially a good idea to buy in an area like that, although it is still a risk. Still, all of that said, maybe 'investment' isn't as important to you as 'enjoyment,' meaning you need to be able to live in the home and enjoy it. Let's take "location," for example. If you have six kids and need a large home in which to live, and you can only afford a big house in a depressed area, then go for it! At least you are the homeowner, and the house is all yours! It will appreciate over time also. It may not appreciate at quite the more elevated levels as the nicer areas of town, but it will still see gains if you hold onto the house long enough.

Now that we've discussed characteristics of homes that can make the resale market potentially more challenging, here is a list of characteristics of what to look FOR when you are out shopping for your first house.

(Keep in mind that this is your first house, and you are likely buying in a more moderate price point. And so the idea that you can get ALL of these things may be misguided. Still, determine which of these are most important to you, and keep them in mind as you tour homes.)

16) LOCATION, LOCATION, LOCATION!! — This is the number one secret to real estate. Buy the least expensive property in the nicest neighborhood. Period. Exclamation point! Why? Well, that's where the potential for appreciation is greatest.
17) VIEWS! — If you have unobstructed views of mountains, park, water, a pretty field of flowers, or any sort of landscape that brings peace and zen to the inhabitants of the home, then that property will be highly sought after in the resale market.
18) Pristine landscaping. — A well-manicured lawn brings a certain calm and order to the "feel" of the home. If you continue to keep it well-manicured while you are the homeowner, it will assist greatly in getting top dollar for the home in the resale market.
19) Spacious modern kitchen. — Remember how I said that when you are entertaining, "everyone ends up in the kitchen." Well, that characteristic right there is absolute key when you go to sell the home one day. The better the kitchen, the easier it will be to sell and the higher price you could likely get!
20) 2 ½ bathrooms. — Two bathrooms is great. But having that one extra half bath for guests brings the property over the line between "nice" and "very nice." And buyers in the resale market

will be willing to pay top dollar for that difference. It may not be possible to get 2 ½ baths for your first home (or even two baths for your first home), but this will be good information for your second home!

21) Two living spaces! — This right here is becoming a BIG deal! Everyone wants to be able to escape from one another in the home. This seems to have become even more pronounced since the Pandemic. Bi-levels and Tri-level floorplans tend to provide this, and luckily they can in the price point for a first-time homebuyer.

22) Ample closet space! — This is especially true of the Primary Bedroom! We all tend to accumulate more "stuff," and so lots of closet space is important for resale.

23) 3-car Garage! — That third bay of a garage is shockingly valuable. The difference in resale value right now at the time of writing this book in my town in Western Colorado is about $40K-50K by just having that third bay for the garage. This may or may not be in your price point as a first-time homebuyer, but it can help you in search criteria for the second home!

24) RV Parking. — Americans are increasingly adding to their repertoire of toys. Campers, boats, ATV's, motorcycles, trailers, you name it! RV Parking is becoming a very hot commodity

in the resale market, and buyers are willing to pay a premium to have it. This will bode very well for you in the resale market, even if you personally don't need it.

25) Outdoor living spaces. — This is another Covid result. People want to be able to BE OUTSIDE! Living outside in your personal outdoor living space is a lifestyle amenity that buyers will pay a pretty penny to have. Even if the house you are looking at buying doesn't have this yet, if there is *room* for you to create it, then that will bode extremely well for you in the resale market. And the more of them you create, the better! Front of the house, side of the house, back of the house, etc. People will pay top-dollar for the property if they can see themselves relaxing in their very own outdoor living spaces.

26) Work-spaces. — Sorry to bring up the Pandemic yet again, but this is yet one more result of it. Back when everyone had to work remotely, they needed space to get away from family, kids, and one-other. If a home has a slightly larger landing at the top of the stairs that could be a workspace for a desk and laptop, or if there is a possible "office nook" area, then this will make the property more desirable for resale. In this day in age, when many people can work from home or work

hybrid, having these work-spaces can make all the difference.
27) Central Air. In Colorado, we have something called an "evaporative cooler." If you are reading this book from Texas, then you likely have no idea what I'm talking about. Long story short, having Central Air is much more desirable than an evaporative cooler. And it's shockingly better for resale.
28) Updated. If a property is already updated, then there is significant value to you there, both in terms of money and time. I'm not saying it's a bad idea to put in sweat equity into a property. Quite the opposite. But you'd have to be able to purchase that property for a lot less money in order to make it worthwhile.
29) Tall or Vaulted Ceilings. A tall ceiling really does differentiate the older homes from the newer ones. Vaulted ceilings make a property seem bigger or more grand. Lower ceilings feel dingy, dark, and limiting. Even if just part of the property provides a vaulted or taller ceiling, then this is a desirable characteristic that will pay you back once you go to sell it.
30) Open Floor Plan. An open floor plan is one in which the kitchen opens to the great room, which opens to the dining spaces, which opens to the outdoor living spaces. It is meant to provide lots of light and a spacious feeling

where you can stretch out, entertain, and feel free. If the property you are thinking of buying does NOT have this, then look to see if walls can be removed to CREATE a more open feel. It could pay you back in dividends when you go to sell it.

31) Laundry Room. It's amazing to me how many million-dollar homes are being built today that don't provide a nice large and bright laundry room. Those homes sit on the market much longer because people WANT a nice big laundry room. A place to hang clothes out of the dryer or to fold them right away. If the laundry room is tight and limiting, the property likely won't bring in as much money when you go to resell it.

32) New Windows. Windows have skyrocketed in price in the last few years. So if you find a property in which the windows are new (or newer), then you will have saved thousands of dollars. Conversely, if the windows are all older, then you are potentially setting yourself up for a giant bill later.

33) New Roof. I cannot stress enough how important this is. Roofs have doubled in cost in the last few years, and that trajectory is not slowing down. Labor and materials are both becoming exponentially more expensive, and a deteriorating roof can be very costly in damage

to the house if there is a leak. Additionally, your homeowner's insurance can be very expensive if the roof is old. Therefore, I advise my clients to give a new roof additional value.

34) New Hot Water Heater and/or New Furnace. The cost of a new hot water heater or a new furnace can be substantial. So if they are new in the home that you are considering buying, then know there is good value there. Conversely, if they are older, then you may end up with a giant price tag that you didn't expect. You may think of Buying a Home Warranty. (I will talk more about Home Warranties in a future chapter.)

35) Foundation. Foundation repair work can cost as little as a thousand dollars and as much as several hundred thousand dollars. And the kicker is that homeowner's insurance doesn't cover it. In other words, a failing foundation could cause you to go into foreclosure if you're not careful. And if that happens, it will mutilate your credit for up to 10 years. THAT's how important it is that you look for jagged cracks in the walls or foundation in a property that you are buying. And if it has them, then have a reputable structural engineer come out to look at it and give you a written evaluation.

Aren't sellers required to disclose all adverse material facts?

Yes, but not all homeowners are knowledgeable about that sort of thing. So "Buyer Beware."

In a court of law, you would have to prove that a Seller intentionally hid a known defect from you, and sometimes that can be a tricky thing to do. And if you've seen the cost of attorneys these days, you could spend your life savings on attorneys and still not see a payout to make it worth it.

This brings us to the topic of Inspections in Chapter 5.

CHAPTER 5

Inspections

In the State of Colorado, an Inspection isn't even a requirement. You can buy a property, and not even have an inspection done at all. (*I don't recommend this.*)

Also in Colorado, inspectors aren't regulated by the Department of Regulatory Agencies (like real estate agents are). So basically, anyone on the street can go have business cards made and call themselves an inspector.

And if all of that isn't bad enough, many home inspectors will make you sign a contract stating that they are not liable if they miss something on the inspection. In other words, you are essentially told that you cannot sue them if they make a mistake.

You CAN sue them, but you may not win.

So, it's crucially important that you get a number of reputable referrals in choosing a home inspector. And most home inspections cost between $300-600, depending on the area and the size and age of the home.

But you aren't finished with inspections after the home inspector does his assessment. There are a number of other inspections that you can also get. It just depends on how much money you are willing to spend, and how important those things are to you.

Of course, I am going to say it's a good idea to get them all. But many first-time homebuyers are struggling just to pay for the approximately $400 initial home inspection. Still, here is an additional list of inspections you *may* consider getting:

1) Sewer scope. Sometimes tree branches and debris will compromise your sewer lines. And if there is a major problem, sewage can back up into your house. This can be significantly damaging to the house (and really gross). And depending on your homeowner's insurance policy, it may or may not be covered by insurance.
2) Septic Assessment. If the house you are buying isn't on sewer, then it's on septic. It's very important to have the septic inspected by a reputable septic company. At a minimum, you are going to want documentation of the last time the septic was pumped and how often it was maintained. If the seller doesn't have those documents, absolutely spend the money to have the septic inspected!
3) Lead Based Paint. In Colorado, a Lead Based Paint disclosure is required for all property built before January 1, 1978. Most buyers waive

the opportunity for a Lead Based Paint assessment. But if Lead Based Paint is worrisome to you, then get the test done. I will say that very few buyers actually have this done. But it doesn't mean that it's not a good idea. You can also purchase your own Lead Based Paint kit at some hardware stores.

4) Asbestos testing. Property that was built back in the 1930's, 40's, 50's, and 60's may or may not have asbestos in the walls and/or the roof. The only way to know for sure is to have it tested. If you are planning to tear out walls or replace the roof, then you will want to know if there is asbestos. Why? Well, first of all, air born asbestos can make you very sick if you ingest the asbestos, and in some cases, it could even cause death. Secondly, asbestos disposal can be very expensive.

5) Methamphetamine testing. If the neighbors report that black paint or foil covered the windows of the property at some point, or if it was ever known to be a "drug house," then you should spend the money to discern if the property was ever used as a narcotics lab (aka "meth lab"). If so, it can make you and the other inhabitants of the home very sick and could cause death. Additionally, methamphetamine removal is extraordinarily expensive. There's a lot more to it than getting new windows and

repainting walls. It requires an industrial hygienist to evaluate and correctly dispose of a number of materials. (Sellers are required to report if the house was ever a meth lab, but sometimes they do not. It is better to double check if you suspect it.)

6) Radon Testing. In Colorado, radon gas is present in a lot of the ground. And it can make you sick or even eventually cause death. Therefore, a radon mitigation system may need to be installed. I highly recommend this test, and if the test reads above the EPA limit, then ask the Seller to install a mitigation system. A mitigation system is currently running $1300-2,000 depending on the location and size of the home.

7) Mill Tailings Analysis and Gamma Radiation (Radiological) Survey. In Western Colorado, a number of homes built before the 1980's were built on top of mill tailings to stabilize the foundation. Mill Tailings are the byproduct of uranium, and it wasn't until the 1980's that the EPA realized how radioactive and toxic they are. The U.S. Department of Energy removed a lot of the mill tailings under thousands of structures. But not all homeowners allowed it. A Mill Tailings Report (requested by your real estate agent and provided for free by the State Health Department) shows whether or not mill

tailings are present in or around the property. If mill tailings are present, then I highly suggest getting a Gamma Radiation (Radiological) Survey to determine if the radioactivity exceeds EPA standards. This is also usually a free test by the State Health Department.

8) Roof Inspection. Although the home inspector should be able to tell if the roof is in good or poor condition, sometimes home inspectors aren't expert enough to truly determine the health of the roof. If the roof is already suspect, sometimes a good idea to get a separate roof inspection. (Additionally, if there is snow on the roof during the inspection, then the inspector may or may not be able to access and evaluate the roof in its entirety.)

9) Foundation Inspection from a Certified Structural Engineer. If there are any cracks in the walls or in the foundation of the property you are considering buying (especially if the cracks are jagged), then I highly suggest getting a written foundation inspection from a certified structural engineer. This will not be a cheap inspection. But the cost of repairing a failing foundation could be as high as hundreds of thousands of dollars. (Again, sellers must disclose if there are any known structural damages to the house. But not all sellers are honest.)

10) Neighbor inspection. I highly recommend driving by the property you are purchasing at all hours of the day. Stop to walk around. Is there an annoying barking dog? Are there loud parties happening on a Saturday night after 10 pm? Knock on the neighbors' doors and meet your future neighbors. How do you feel about them? All of this is going to matter greatly to you once you are the homeowner.
11) Insurance Review. We will talk more about homeowners' insurance in a later chapter, but what's most important in this section is that you tell your insurance agent the address of the house you are buying. That way the insurance agent can look up the property to see if there were ever any major claims against it, such as flooding or a leak in the roof or worse. Although sellers are supposed to disclose everything, the fact is that sometimes they don't. An examination of insurance claims on the house will tell you if you need to be able to ask questions or require documentation that the property was properly remediated and repaired by licensed contractors who knew what they were doing.
12) Mold Inspection or "Infrared Inspection." Although it's yet one more additional expense, you can have the property tested for mold and/or moisture. Certain types of mold can

make you very sick, and so it's good to know if those mold spores are present (or could become present due to moisture). If there is, then try to get the Seller to pay for mold remediation, which can get expensive depending on the severity. Again, sellers must disclose if they know of any known mold, but some sellers don't even know if there is.

After you've finished all of your inspections, you and your real estate agent will create an Inspection Objection list. These are the things you are saying that you want for the Seller to repair or replace. A few days later, you will receive a document called an Inspection Resolution that will detail the items that the Seller is willing to repair or replace. And then you will decide from there if you want to continue forward with the purchase or not.

Sometimes it's a good idea to purchase a Home Warranty. You may be able to get the Seller to pay for it, or you may decide to pay for one yourself. A Home Warranty covers items such as the hot water heater, appliances, and sometimes they will cover the furnace and air conditioning units. It just depends on which Home Warranty is purchased, and the warranty lasts for usually one year, although you can buy warranties that last up to two years (and some are renewable each year.) They range in cost from $500-900 or so.

If you can, it's a good idea to include a Home Warranty in the Inspection Objection. That way you don't have to pay for it, but you have a peace-of-mind for at least for first year of home-ownership.

CHAPTER 6

Off Record Matters

Off Record Matters sounds boring, right? Well, it's actually pretty important.

Off Record Matters includes all the information not necessarily provided in the title work. We will discuss the title commitment in a future chapter, but for now, let's talk about all the things you don't realize that you needed to know. That's essentially "off record matters" in a nutshell.

For example, it's a good idea to determine if there are any Registered Sex Offenders living near the house that you are considering buying.

Also, what is the future land use for the properties surrounding the home you are looking at buying? Are they going to be building a new Walgreens behind it? How do you feel about that? Or are they going to be building an elementary school with several school zones. How do you feel about that?

What if the future plan is to build a homeless shelter down the block from your house? Or a jail? Are you going to be okay with that?

What if there is a giant noisy highway that is planned to be built right behind your house!

It's just important to be informed on what sorts of developments are planned in the future near the property you are considering buying.

A phone call to the county and/or city Planning Department will answer those questions. Again, they are off record matters. And they can be very important in your decision-making process when buying your first home.

CHAPTER 7

Title Commitment

The most important thing for me to tell you about a Title Commitment is that you will want to pay especially focused attention on the Exceptions section. This tells you what the title company WILL NOT be ensuring with regard to the title of the property.

- Title insurance is the document that grants you the ownership of the property.

You will also need to know if there are any weird clouds on the title that need to be removed so that you are getting "clear title" to the property. For example, is there a mechanic's lien against the property because the Seller never paid the flooring contractor? Is there an IRS lien against the property because the Seller is 10 years behind on their income taxes?

The purpose of a Title Commitment is to verify ownership of the real estate that is legitimately given to the homebuyer. Essentially, it ensures that the Seller has the right to sell the property to the Buyer. It also lets you and the mortgage lender know if there is "clear title."

Title Commitment

Who pays for the title commitment? Well, it depends on what is stated in the contract. If you Google that question for Colorado, it will tell you that the Buyer pays for the title commitment. But in the county in which I live, it is actually generally the Seller who pays for it. Either way, it depends on what the contract states as to who pays for the title commitment, usually $1200-$3000 or so, depending on the price of the home.

Title can be taken in three different ways (in Colorado):

1) If a single person is buying the property, then they take title as Tenancy in Severalty.
2) If a married couple is buying a home, then they are going to want the right of survivorship if, God forbid, one of them deceases. So, they would take title as Joint Tenants.
3) Lastly, if two buddies decide to buy a house together, they may want to take title as Tenant in Common instead. That way, each of them owns a particular percentage of the property, and upon death of one of the tenants, their percentage passes to the deceased person's heirs or beneficiaries.

The other function that the title company provides is that they are oftentimes the holder of the earnest money.

What is earnest money? Earnest money is the amount of money the Seller is requiring for you to put toward the purchase to prove that you are serious. If you change your mind on buying the property after all of the contingencies of the contract are met, then you could lose your earnest money.

(Check with your real estate agent for a list of all of those contingency deadline dates.)

So earnest money is serious business.

The good news is that if you find too many things wrong with the property during inspection, or if you are concerned about Due Diligence documents or Off Record Matters, then you can get your earnest money back as long as it's before the deadlines. So keep all those deadlines in mind as well.

Do you get the earnest money back at Closing? Well, it depends. Most people allow their earnest money to go toward the down payment. But in a VA loan or a USDA loan, sometimes people opt to have their earnest money refunded to them because their down payment is zero dollars. You will work this part out with your lender and real estate agent.

(We will discuss types of loans in a future chapter.)

A few days before Closing, the title company is the entity that will be working with your real estate agent and lender such that all of the numbers on the Buyer's

Settlement Statement are correct. Your Closer at the title company will be in constant direct contact with you, your agent, and your loan officer.

So feel free to ask the Closer clarifying questions, both on the title commitment and on the Buyer's Settlement Statement. And you should be able to ask your real estate agent and lender those questions as well.

HORROR STORY 4:

Early in my career as a real estate agent two decades ago, someone reached out to me to list their house. They invited me inside and showed me all around the house. They were very knowledgeable about the property, and we signed a listing contract. Come to find out later that it was actually the renter who had signed the listing contract. She had pretended to be the Seller, and signed the actual property owner's name as if it was her own. Thankfully I caught it before we went live in the MLS. But eventually the title company would have caught it too. One of the purposes of the title company is to ensure that the Seller really is who they say they are. Real estate fraud is much more prevalent than the general public realizes.

Title fraud is an ever-growing problem currently in the United States. Therefore, the title company you use should be reputable and thorough.

CHAPTER 8

Due Diligence Documents and Surveys

The title of this chapter doesn't sound very exciting, does it? Well, what if there is an easement running through your property that will allow utility companies to be on your property when you least expect it?

Or what if you had planned on digging a pool for fun pool parties on the property, but an easement will prevent it?

What if the property has solar panels, but you have no idea who is responsible for maintaining them or whether or not they are paid off? What if at Closing, it's your responsibility to take over the $25,000 solar panel lease for the next 30 years?

These are examples of *Due Diligence Documents.*

Other examples are the HOA documents, not just the CC&R's (the Community Covenants and Restrictions), but also the notes of the latest meeting and the financials of the HOA.

What if the neighbors hate and argue with one another ad nauseam at the HOA meetings, and the neighborhood just isn't a friendly place in which to live? Unless you receive and actually read the notes from the latest meeting, you won't know this so that you can make a decision if you really want to live there.

What if the HOA decided that everyone must buy the most expensive tile roof and that all the roofs must match within the next 2 years? What if your roof doesn't need to be replaced for 10 more years, but now this HOA rule will require you to replace it in 2 years?

You better have read your HOA meeting notes so that you know whether or not you really want to buy that house in that neighborhood.

What if the HOA has misappropriated funds and is out of money when there is a costly problem with the neighborhood irrigation pond. And now the HOA is going to need to collect a $500 Special Assessment from each homeowner to pay for it. Do you really want to buy that house knowing that?

This is why it's important to receive and read the financial statement and the Annual Budget of the HOA.

Now let's talk about *Surveys*. Sometimes a survey will already be included in the title work or the due diligence documents. And sometimes surveys will be required to be done.

What is a survey? It's a document that provides information as to where the boundary lines of the property run.

That said, there are two documents that can provide this information. There is an *Improvement Location Certificate* (or ILC), which can be required by the title company or the lender if improvements were made to the property, such as a new structure. An ILC will cost between $200-500.

The other is a full *Survey*, which can be more costly. These are used when there is a boundary line adjustment or dispute or if a neighboring property is encroaching onto the property you are buying. It is best to get the Seller to pay for this due to the potential cost.

Surveys will provide information regarding easements on the property and other information. It is important that you understand what you are buying and any potential future issues you could have with the property.

HORROR STORY 5:

Upon receiving the ILC with the title work of a 1964-built property that my buyer was buying, we saw that the next-door neighbor's garage was encroaching by 50 feet onto the property that the buyer was buying. It was a significant encroachment. The title company was willing to go through with the Closing, but it identified the encroachment as an "exception" to the title commitment. After Closing, my buyer promptly hired an attorney and filed a lawsuit on the neighbor. He required that she either demolish her garage, or else agree to a boundary line adjustment that gave him a 1/3 acre of her lot in exchange for her being able to keep her garage. He also required her to pay for the $3,000 survey that was needed for the boundary line adjustment to be approved by the county. Had the neighbor NOT agreed, then she would've had to have torn down her big, beautiful garage. So she agreed to the survey cost and the boundary line adjustment. (I will say that his swift legal action on the neighbor after closing shocked me, but it worked out because what he really wanted was a larger lot. And that boundary line adjustment gave it to him. I felt badly for the neighbor, though.

But to be fair, she bought a house that encroached on the neighbor's property, and there is liability with that.

Unfortunately, she didn't seem aware of the encroachment, and she paid dearly for that.)

CHAPTER 9

Appraisals

An *appraisal* is essentially an in-depth home valuation that compares the home value to a number of other sales of similar properties in the area. It is meant to provide evidence to the lender that the property is worth the dollar amount that is being lent on the property.

Most first-time home buyers get a mortgage loan, and so the lender is likely going to require an appraisal on the property. I highly recommend waiting until you get through all of the inspections, off record matters deadlines, HOA documents deadlines and title deadlines before you order and pay for an appraisal.

Appraisals can cost upwards of $700, and you aren't going to want to pay the appraisal fee if you decide to terminate on one of the other prior contingencies.

The loan officer will order the appraisal, and so that it not something that you will have to do. But hear me on this. Loan officers can get a little overzealous and order an appraisal right away as soon as you go under contract.

Your lender might not know that you want to wait on ordering the appraisal, and so you and your real estate agent will need to be clear with them that they NEED TO WAIT!

Otherwise, if things fall apart on inspection, you may end up paying $700 for an appraisal on a property that you aren't even buying anymore.

Again, what is the reason for the appraisal?

Well, it tells the lender whether or not the property is actually worth what you said you would pay for it. For example, let's say that you got into a bidding war on a property listed at $400,000, and you agreed to pay $430,000 for it.

If the appraisal comes in at $405,000 instead, then there is a $25,000 "*appraisal gap.*"

1)   An *appraisal gap* occurs when the appraisal value comes in lower than the price at which the property is under contract.

This means that the lender won't loan you the entirety of the money you will need to buy the house. And so unless you are willing to pay the "appraisal gap," then you cannot buy the property at that $430,00 price.

It is possible, however, that your real estate agent can negotiate the price down to the appraised value of $405,000. Or maybe the seller will be willing to "split the appraisal gap" with you.

It just depends on a number of factors.

It's possible that either your real estate agent or the listing agent can provide "comps" to the appraiser that support the higher $430,000 price tag. A *comp* is recent sale of a property that is similar to the one you are buying. Sometimes appraisers don't realize that there are additional comps that they should have considered. And depending on the appraiser, the appraiser may be willing to consider the additional comps, and change their opinion of value.

Appraisals are a tricky thing sometimes. What you DON'T want to happen is to have paid $400 for a home inspection and $700 for an appraisal, and then the appraisal comes in so low that you cannot get a loan on the property. You would be out $1100 if that were to happen.

So it's important that your real estate agent is able to have confidence in the price you are paying for the property.

Many people understandably confuse the inspection and the appraisal. Let me clarify: The *home inspection* is something that you order. You shop for the right inspector, and you hire him/her to tell you all about the house. He/she will explain what needs to be fixed or repaired and what is in good shape.

The appraiser doing an *appraisal*, however, will be hired by the loan officer on your behalf. You may have to pay for the appraisal up front or maybe after the appraisal is ordered. Sometimes you can pay for the appraisal at closing too. It just depends. And the appraisal is an opinion of value backed up by sales comps.

The appraiser also conducts an "inspection" of their own.

If you get an FHA or VA loan, then the appraiser will "inspect" items like the roof and foundation and check for peeling paint and broken windows. Those items have to be repaired in order for the house to close. Who pays for those repairs is up to the negotiating power of your real estate agent. It may be you who pays, or it may be the Seller who pays.

I once had an FHA appraiser require a kitchen sink faucet to be vented. The appraiser also happened to be a master plumber, and he made that a requirement before we could close.

If items on the appraisal are flagged for repair, then the appraiser will need to come out a second time for a "recheck" after that repair. And although you already paid $700 for the appraisal, the recheck will cost upwards of another $250.

So appraisals can get expensive. And if you don't have the money for the repairs, and if the Seller isn't willing to do them, then the contract will terminate, and you will be out upwards of $1100 for the appraisal and inspection.

This is where the prowess and skill of your real estate agent will come into play. A savvy real estate agent will hire out the work to be completed and paid for at Closing, possibly out of Seller Proceeds and even possibly at the expense of the agent. This happens more than you would expect.

So going back to the earlier part of the book ... It is imperative that you hire the right real estate agent who has a proven track record of completing a significant number of transactions. Usually, those agents don't see FHA repair items as a deal killer. They still find a way to make it happen for their clients.

CHAPTER 10

Loans

In Chapter 8, I threw around terms like FHA loan and VA loan, and you may have no idea what I was talking about. Lending can get complicated, but I am going to try to break it down in simple terms here.

These are generally the types of loans used by First Time Home Buyers:

1) *Conventional Loan 20% Down* — This loan generally requires a higher credit score, and if you were able to save 20% down, then you won't have to pay for something referred to as "MI" or Mortgage Insurance.

2) (Mortgage Insurance provides insurance to the lender in case the borrower defaults on their loan, but if you are putting down 20%, then the likelihood of you defaulting is very low. Therefore, you don't have to pay for mortgage insurance.

3) *Conventional Loan 5% Down* – This loan also generally requires a higher credit score, but you only have to save 5% of the purchase price of the house for it. Unfortunately, though, you

may also have to pay the Mortgage Insurance (MI) in some cases, which equates to approximately $300/month or so. (Lately there have been 3% conventional mortgages too. So sometimes lenders will have new and innovative loan products depending on your credit score and the type of property you are buying. It just depends.)

4) *FHA Loan* – This is the loan used most often with First Time Home Buyers. It only requires 3.5% down and doesn't normally require as high of a credit score as a Conventional loan. It does require Mortgage Insurance (MI), however. So be ready for that. (*CHFA loan* – A CHFA loan is sometimes a loan option for First Time Home Buyers. It generally only requires $1,000 down, and you have to take an 8-hour CHFA First Time Home Buyer class either in the classroom or online. The class is actually excellent, and only having to save $1,000 for the down payment is a big draw to this loan for first time home buyers. But generally the interest rate, closing costs, and Mortgage Insurance (MI) are higher with this type of loan. So go in with your eyes open on that.)

5) *VA Loan* – This is a loan for military veterans who served long enough to qualify for their VA benefit. VA loans require zero down payment,

usually have much lower interest rates, and they have lower closing costs. This is how we as a society repay our veterans who put themselves in harm's way to sacrifice for our country. The only downside to getting a VA loan is that the VA Appraiser is very strict! Any peeling paint, roof issues, broken windows, and a myriad of other requirements must be ameliorated before this loan will be approved. Some sellers or listing agents don't like to accept offers with VA loans because of this reason. So be sure you know who is going to be willing to pay to make those repairs if they exist. (I should also add that sometimes a VA funding fee is required for non-disabled veterans. Just ask your loan officer for more information.)

6) *USDA Loan* – This is a loan for property in rural areas. It requires zero money down, which makes it an enticing loan. Sometimes it can also have lower interest rates too! But it does generally require Mortgage Insurance (MI). You just have to determine if it's the right loan for you if you are buying in a rural area.

Although there are lots of other variations of loans, these are generally the five most widely used. Up until recently, the mortgage rate was much lower on a Conventional Loan than on an FHA loan, but that is no longer necessarily the case. At the time of writing this book, the government has done some weird things that appear backwards.

I now have buyers with really high credit scores who are going FHA on their loans (instead of Conventional) because the mortgage rate is lower. It's strange.

You would think that the loan requiring the higher credit score (Conventional) would have the lower mortgage rates. And it's always been that way until the last couple of years.

Although our heads are exploding in the industry as we try to wrap our minds around it, we have come to accept that the mortgage rate will fluctuate daily depending on a number of factors. The key is to have an exceptional mortgage loan officer who has their hand on the pulse of it every minute of everyday.

In other words, mortgage companies and even loan officers can vary wildly depending on their prowess and standing in the industry. They are definitely not all created equal!

Again, the right real estate agent should be able to help you with some outstanding referrals in this regard. And it is why I highly recommend using a local lender with an exceptional reputation.

CHAPTER 11

Seller Concessions and Rate Buy-downs

Every loan has closing costs. Some lenders require the borrower to pay $5,000 in closing costs while others are upwards of $10,000 in closing costs. But I've also seen closing costs as low as $3700. Again, not all lenders are created equal.

So it's important to ask your loan officer how much your closing costs will be.

Why does this matter so much? Well, because you are going to have to bring THAT dollar amount to the closing table along WITH your down payment. And that can feel like a lot of money out of your pocket.

At the time of writing this book, it is oftentimes possible to wrap the closing costs into the purchase price of the house such that the Seller pays your closing costs instead. We call this *"Seller Concessions."* But you will have to have an upward trending real estate market to do that.

If the market trends downward, then it makes it much harder for this to work because the property has to appraise for the purchase price plus the closing costs.

This sort of thinking can also apply to mortgage rate *buy-downs*. That is, if your real estate agent can negotiate for you such that the Seller pays both your closing costs AND perhaps a one percent rate buy-down, then that is optimum. Then your mortgage rate will be one percent lower than the actual mortgage rate, which brings down your monthly payment.

There are all sorts of rate buy-down options out there, and it is important that you explore them with your loan officer and your real estate agent together to discern the best one for you.

Unfortunately, if you are buying a house in a high-demand Sellers Market, then this can become very difficult to do. In other words, if there are lots of Buyers who want to buy the house that you do, then the Sellers likely won't be paying for your closing costs on your loan or a rate buy down.

So everything just depends on the property itself, the timing of the market, the negotiating prowess of your real estate agent, the seller's urgency to sell (or lack thereof), and the listing agent's attitude toward rate buy-downs and seller concessions.

CHAPTER 12

A Buyer's market versus A Seller's Market

A *Buyer's Market* is when the market conditions are more favorable to the buyer, and a *Sellers' Market* occurs when the market conditions are more favorable to the Seller.

From 2020 to 2023, we were in a fierce Sellers' Market. There weren't enough homes on the market to support the unprecedented demand from Buyers to buy those homes. We saw scores of bidding wars, bidding up prices from a few thousand dollars to as much as hundreds of thousands of dollars, depending on the area and price point of the home. (I even had a client whose house in San Francisco bided up $1 million!)

During that buying frenzy, Sellers got to choose the highest and best offers while buyers lost out on home after home after home. It was like nothing we'd ever seen before, and many home prices skyrocketed to values double that what they were before the Pandemic.

If you are about to ask how could THAT happen with appraisers needing to value the homes at the value of those contracts, that's a great question! Well, many of the buyers who actually won those bidding wars were cash buyers and investors. And a cash buyer doesn't need an appraisal.

In those days, if you were a buyer who needed a loan to buy a house, then in many cases, you had to be willing to pay the *"appraisal gap."* Remember how we talked about the Appraisal Gap in Chapter 9?

The result of all the craziness was that home prices surged 35-60% in most of the country. Some places saw 100-200% increases! Don't you know that homeowners during that time period were very glad they owned homes.

Renters lost out on all that beautiful equity, and then rental rates skyrocketed to boot. Renters endured a double whammy while homeowners enjoyed a very fast-growing wealth practically overnight.

But once mortgage rates began to increase in the middle of 2022, the housing market began to shift, and home price appreciation has leveled out during the time that I am writing this book. Some areas of the country are still seeing modest appreciation while others are seeing some price drops. Yet some of the country is still seeing fierce bidding wars and crazy appreciation levels.

Currently people are hoping for a Buyers' Market soon, but due to scarcity of the supply of homes and the likelihood of mortgage rates declining over the course of 2024, some economists believe that we could end up with another buying frenzy by the end of the year.

Still, let's talk about a time in which we saw a beautiful Buyers' Market.

After the Crash of '08, we had a very large surplus of homes for sale all over the country. It was traumatic for Sellers, but Buyers could have their pick and practically name their price!

My buyers oftentimes viewed 30-70 homes before they decided on which one they wanted to buy. And once they decided, then we oftentimes were able to negotiate down the price by $10,000-100,000 depending on the property.

To put that into perspective, during the time in which I am writing this book in 2024, my Buyers usually look at 5-30 homes before they decide which one they want. It's becoming more of a normal market.

Many would argue that we are somewhere nearing equilibrium in the market we are in now. Equilibrium is when the number of buyers and the number of listings are equal.

It's not quite equal yet, but we are getting there.

So it's not a Buyers' Market or a Sellers' Market. Some would even call it a bipolar market. That's because some homes sit on the market for 90-120 days while others are gone in 24 hours. It just depends on the desired features of the home, the list price, and the level of marketing used by the listing agent.

If a home has a number of the desired features that I listed in Chapter 4, then it won't be on the market for very long in a healthy market in which we are potentially reaching equilibrium. In fact, you might even see a bidding war on it if the listing agent has the prowess and skill to get one going on it.

(I am currently writing a book entitled, "Cindy Says: The SMART Way to Sell your Home." And that's where I talk about how to get *bidding wars* going on the home you intend to sell.)

Somebody once asked me *how* to "time the market" in buying a house. And although I do study data daily such that I can tell you what is currently happening and what I believe will happen as long as all other variables remain constant, the truth is that not all variables always remain constant.

What do I mean by that?

Well, we just don't know what is going to happen in the global geo-political economy. For example, if the cost of energy is high because of OPEC, wars, or even domestic political decisions, then the prices of goods become higher. This inflation is met with higher interest rates which basically circuitously results in higher mortgage rates.

But if the cost of energy becomes lower, then if you use this line of thinking, then mortgage rates become lower.

But if you buy a house at a high mortgage rate, then you can always refinance the house once rates decrease. And if you hold onto the house for 3-5 years (depending on the geopolitical factors), generally people experience appreciation resulting in some nice equity.

But if you buy a house one year, and then decide to sell it the next year, chances are you haven't seen enough appreciation to pay for the cost to sell the house. Costs to sell include title insurance, tax certificate, transfer fees, taxes, commissions, etc. Unless you owned the house during 2020 or 2021 (during record appreciation), it is likely you will be eating into your down payment to pay all those costs to sell.

Some Sellers who only had a modest down payment would be upside down if they were to sell after only one year. It just depends on the market conditions.

But if you hold onto the house 3-5 years or more, then chances are that you will have enough equity to sell the house and walk away with a potentially impressive check at closing.

Just this week I am selling a property for $100,000 more than what my Buyer paid for it 4 years ago. He was a first-time homebuyer back then, and he is ecstatic to receive his big fat check. I also have a seller who bought a house a year ago (in 2023), and prices haven't appreciated high enough for him to be able to sell yet. Case in point, you really need to be able to hold onto your house for 3-5 years to give enough time for the property to appreciate.

Even my clients who bought at the top of the market before the Crash of '08 have now experienced enough appreciation such that their homes have doubled in value by 2024. They had to wait 10 years for it to re-appreciate to the price they paid for it and then another 6 years for it to double in value. But believe me, they are very glad that they held onto those homes.

My point is that if you hold onto a property for a longer length of duration, then that investment has historically seen great gains.

Think of the couple who bought a house in 1970 for $25,000 at a mortgage rate of 7% back then. That same house is now worth between $450,000-1,000,000 depending on the location, home features, and the updating that was done since 1970. Not a bad investment! And the cherry on top is that they got to live in it and make it their home all that time.

So whether or not you are in a Buyers' Market or a Sellers' Market when you buy your home, the important part is that you became a homeowner, took good care of it, and held onto it for a few years. And it's YOURS!

CHAPTER 13

Utilities and Insurance

The title of this chapter sounds boring as heck. But it's actually the crucial part that a lot of real estate agents forget to explain to their first-time homebuyers.

And then buyers walk into their new home and the lights won't turn on. Or the water isn't running. Or their internet isn't set up. Or suddenly the irrigation line busted and water is pouring into the basement. Who is going to pay for the damage?

Now suddenly Utilities and Insurance sounds captivating, right?

Okay, now that I have your attention on this, you need to set up these things before Closing:

1) Electricity and Gas. (Sometimes they are paid to the same utility company and sometimes they are separate. Ask your real estate agent.)
2) Water. (Sometimes the title company will transfer it for you, and sometimes you have to set it up separately. Sometimes it's the HOA who sets it up for you. Ask your real estate agent.)

3) Internet. (Many times you will need to set this up a couple of weeks in advance. Ask your real estate agent or the neighbors who they like to use for this.)
4) Cable. (I know cable is a dying breed, but some generations still like to get it. If you are one of them, you will want to set this up a couple of weeks in advance of closing.)
5) Sewer. (Oftentimes the title company will switch the sewer into your name for you. Just ask your real estate agent for sure.)
6) Trash and Recycling. (Sometimes there are several options for who to use for trash and recycling services. Ask your real estate agent.)
7) Mail. (Be sure to fill out a Change of Address form at the post office or online. It can take up to a couple of weeks for this change to go through, and so you will want to do this ASAP after you get through all the contingencies in the purchase contract.)
8) Solar. (If there is a lease on the solar panels, then you are going to want to apply to have the least changed into your name likely 30 days before closing, according to most solar companies. They will run your credit and determine if they will accept the transfer. But if you are in a Buyer's Market, then I would strongly encourage you to negotiate to have that solar lease paid at closing by the Seller.

Some of those leases run 20-30 years, and it can complicate and make re-selling the home potentially difficult if you sell in a Buyer's Market.)

As for homeowner's insurance, not all insurance companies are created equal. Be careful. Some insurance companies are ridiculously expensive while others are super cheap (and sometimes you get what you pay for.)

Shop around. What you DON'T want to happen is for that insurance company to not cover your home when you need them most. You will need your policy to be bound to your loan by the Insurance Objection date in the contract.

HORROR STORY 6:

Back in 2016, I had some Buyers who did the Final Walkthrough the day before Closing, which is common. (I'll explain Final Walkthroughs in a minute.). But at the Final Walkthrough, the house looked impeccable. Beautiful! A little dated, but not too bad. It was backed up to a park and mountain views, and the buyers were so excited!

It was an unexpectedly cold night that night before closing, though. Actually really cold!

We closed early the next morning, and then the happy new homeowners met the movers at the house. When they walked inside, their eyes grew wide open and their mouths fell open.

The evaporative cooler lines had frozen and burst, and water leaked all night into the ceiling that had since caved in on much of the house. There was water and drywall all over the hardwood floors, all over the kitchen, all over everything. Pretty much everything had to be remediated and replaced.

The ceiling. The walls. The floor. The damaged kitchen cabinets and countertops. Everything!

Thankfully we were sure to have the homeowner's insurance policy in force for the day of closing. And thankfully the Buyers had a good insurance company who paid to put them in a hotel that night, and into a short-term rental property for months thereafter.

The house had to be essentially gutted throughout the main area of the home. The homeowner's insurance policy paid for all of the remediation and repairs, and my clients were able to hand pick all new modern finishes for an incredible new kitchen, new hardwood floors, new everything! Once it was done, it was as if they got a whole new house!

But can you imagine had they not had their insurance in place? Can you imagine if they would've had a cheap insurance company that refused to pay out?

It matters. And you are going to want to be covered if the unexpected happens.

So what is a *Final Walkthrough*? A Final Walkthrough is just that. It's the final time that you will see the property before you go to the closing table to sign documents that transfers title from the Seller to you, the Buyer. It's partly a ceremonious experience while also being sure that the property is in the condition you expect. It's a chance to be sure that inspection items were completed, and it gives me a chance to take celebration photos of the Buyers inside their new home.

Most agents conduct a Final Walkthrough a few days before Closing. Some do it the day before.

And sometimes they do it on the day of Closing if schedules and time permits. I generally try to do it on the day of Closing, right before going to the Closing table.

CHAPTER 14

Closing Day

Your loan officer and your real estate agent should be able to provide you with (and explain) the Buyer's Settlement Statement and Closing Disclosure that shows your bottom-line amount of money that you will need to bring to Closing.

You will either bring a Cashier's Check in that amount (usually made out to the the title company), or you will have already needed to coordinate a wire transfer from your bank on the day before Closing.

I strongly suggest that you do not try to send the wire on the day *of* closing. If your funds are not at the closing table on the day of Closing, then the Seller has the option to keep your earnest money and sell the house to someone else. This doesn't happen often, but it *can*. So it's important that you know and understand that.

You will need a picture ID (usually a government issued Driver's License) for Closing so that the Closer/Notary can verify that you are who you say are.

Sometimes people bring gifts at Closing as part of the celebration of the Closing Day. And depending on how they do Closings in your state, you may be sitting at the closing table with the Sellers also. This is a perfect chance to be able to ask Sellers any questions that you may have, such as:

1) When is trash day?
2) In a community mailbox, which mailbox belongs to that house?
3) What is the code to the garage door, and do they have instructions for how to change it?

These are the most common questions that Buyers ask of Sellers at the Closing table.

In some states and in some situations, we do something called, *"Split Closings,"* in which the Buyers and Sellers close at different times. And sometimes Sellers close remotely if they are already moved to their next destination. If that's the case, then you will want to ask questions like the ones above *before* Closing.

Expect that the Closing will take anywhere from 30 minutes to 90 minutes, depending on the size of the loan package, the speed of the Closer, and how detailed you are in reading the Closing documents.

This is a very exciting day! Some buyers like to take photos with signs that say "I bought a house!" And these are usually provided by the title company. For safety reasons, people like to post these photos on social media, rather than photos of themselves in front of the house itself. (You may not want to tell the whole world the exact address of where you live.)

Closing Day is just one of those special days in life that you'll never forget!

CHAPTER 15

Being SMART

I titled this book, "How to Buy a House the SMART Way" for a reason. Not only should you go into the process being informed, but you also should be able to measure your success so that you feel confident about the largest purchase you'll have ever made (up until this point in your life.)

Back when I was a School Principal, the State of Colorado required every public school to write a School Improvement Plan. And at least back then, we used to talk a lot about *SMART goals*.

SMART goals became all the rage in the business world too. And there's a reason for that. They make sense! They keep you on track! And they help you to know if you have actually succeeded!

That said, you should also be SMART in how you buy a house!

So what is a SMART goal? They are goals that have to be *Specific*, *Measurable*, Attainable, *Results-oriented*, and have a thoughtful *Timetable*.

So let's apply that to the home buying process.

First, be *SPECIFIC* about the house you want! If you don't know what you want, you could end up buying something that you realize later you didn't really want.

Spend the time to really jot down all the things you are looking for, and share it with your real estate agent. List those *"Must Have's"* in order of importance. You'd be surprised how much this is going to help you.

Secondly, write a *MEASUREABLE* goal, such as: "Out of the ten criteria listed in my 'Must Have's List,' the house I choose will have at least 6 of 10 of them."

"But WAIT?" Aren't you supposed to get ALL of them?!

This is the hard part for first-time homebuyers. Many times they are in a lower price point, and it's simply not *ATTAINABLE* to get 100% of your Must Have's.

You have to remember that this is only your first house. You will likely live in it, improve it, and sell it within 3-5 years, and you'll use that equity to *"buy up."* And then in the second house, you'll get more of your Must Have's. And then in the third house, you'll get even more.

And your Must Have's List will change as you grow older and realize more of what's important to you, and what's not.

For example, in my mid 30's, I built a new home on 2-acres. It's what I thought I wanted. Now I live in a lock-n-leave house on 1/8 of an acre because I realized that

I didn't want to have to take care of 2 acres of land. My Must Have's List has evolved and changed completely since then.

Anyhow, once you are honest with yourself about what is *ATTAINABLE* at a certain price point, and you've decided on a property on which to write an offer, ask yourself if you achieved the desired *RESULT* of what you were looking for.

Lastly, decide on the *TIMETABLE* for when you would like to close on that property. Most escrow periods in Colorado tend to be 30 days. In California, it's closer to 60 days.

Sometimes the best thing to do is to have your real estate agent call the listing agent to ask what timetable is best for the Seller. That could be worth its weight in gold if you are in a bidding war for the property, or if you are trying to get them to do a rate buy-down for you.

If you are accommodating to the Seller's timetable, then you might be able to maneuver a better scenario for yourself also.

No matter what, being SMART in your home buying journey will be crucial to ensuring your success. That way on Closing Day, you will be elated to be a new homeowner!!

You'll feel good and confident, and you'll feel like you just won the SuperBowl. THAT's the feeling you want! THAT's when you know ... YOU DID IT!!!

HORROR STORY 7:

Back in late 2019 before the Pandemic, I had a first-time homebuyer who couldn't wrap his head around the type of property that was ATTAINABLE at his price point. We probably looked at 50 houses, in search of 100% of what he was looking for. He later decided just to rent for a year, and start looking again later. By the end of 2020, prices had skyrocketed, and he discovered that he could buy even less of what he had wanted. So he decided to wait another year, and by the end of 2021, prices of first-time homes had essentially doubled in cost. He paid a heavy price for waiting to buy, and it all stemmed from his inability to adjust to what is ATTAINABLE at a particular price point.

Had he bought that first home in 2019, he easily would've grown enough equity that he could have "bought up" to his next home in 2021 and gotten 100% of what he wanted. Instead, he was still just a renter who had spent the last 2 years building equity for someone else instead of for himself.

CHAPTER 16

About me

I promised you in the Introduction that I would tell you more about me, but I wanted for this book to be about **YOU** and YOUR home buying journey. And not about me. So that's why I wrote the whole thing before really telling you much about myself.

I've been selling real estate for the better part of two decades. It was before cell phones were smart phones, before texting, before Siri and GPS, and before e-signatures were a thing. In other words, the world has changed a lot since I started selling real estate.

I was an Assistant Principal (but only paid as a teacher) when I first started into my real estate career. I had difficulty getting ahead financially without a second job. After my normal job at the school, I worked retail on nights and weekends at minimum wage. I also did gift wrap during Christmas Break, although I wasn't very good at it. And I tutored kids and did anything I could to try and make a little extra money.

I had two master's degrees by that point in my life, and I loved what I did working with kids. I loved teaching, mentoring, and making a positive difference. But making the mortgage each month was really hard, and

I sometimes wondered if I should just fall back on my Business degree that I'd earned as an Undergrad.

And that's when I met Sharon Vaughn. Sharon was a "top producer" (high performing agent) at Coldwell Banker. She was ranked #1 in the MLS, and she was the sweetest and most business savvy human I'd ever met. She hired me to "*call on feedback*," or call buyers agents who had shown her listings, and then provide that feedback to her Sellers.

Sharon sat in the office beside mine, and there was an open window between the two offices. And so I could listen to her make phone calls and do deals. She was amazing!!

I asked her if I could go with her on her listing appointments, just to watch. Again, she was mesmerizing to me. She worked with such ease and kindness while also being a bulldog for her clients with a prowess I cannot even articulate in words. She was, and still is, the best real estate agent I've ever known. And she's one of the best humans to have ever walked the planet too.

Sharon passed away from cancer years later, and tears are dropping on my keyboard right now as I type this. But because of her, I am the success story that I am.

After she passed away, I wanted to share with others the gift of real estate that Sharon had bestowed on me. So I organized and taught classes at night to aspiring real estate agents and to people in the community who were just starting to think about buying their first home.

I sold a lot of real estate all those years too, and always made the top 5% in the MLS ranking ... while also serving as either a School Principal or a Teacher. That's right, I worked 2-3 jobs full time until May of 2019.

I had $6 million in volume under contract that May of 2019 while I was also trying to finalize report cards for over 100 kids. (I was teaching Business classes full time to high schoolers at that point.)

I'd hit a point in which I couldn't do both jobs anymore, and I resigned from the school district. It was a devastating decision because I loved my students. I loved teaching. I loved making a difference.

But I also loved selling real estate, and I was able to save for my son's college education because of it. So in June of 2019, I began selling real estate as my one and only full time job.

In 2020, I sold over $22 million in sales volume and earned "Salesperson of the Year!" I earned it again in 2022, and I was inducted into the Chairman's Club for Coldwell Banker in 2023. I also made "International President's Elite," which ranked me in the Top 1% internationally among 100,000 agents and 40 countries.

I started writing this book because I miss teaching. I miss making a difference that might make someone else's life better somehow. It is paying forward what Sharon Vaughn did for me.

And so I decided writing books may provide for that chance.

I sincerely hope this book did that for you. And I would love to know if it did. My contact information is on the next page, and please don't hesitate to email me or call me or write a review of the book.

I am sure that after publishing that I will think of all sorts of things that I should've included in this book, and so I imagine there will be revised editions in the future. Plus, markets are always changing, buyers' needs and sellers' needs are always changing, technology is always changing, and real estate law is always changing.

To my clients of the last two decades, I cannot even tell you how much you mean to me.

Thank you for giving me the chance to earn your business. Thank you for sharing your lives and families with me.

Thank you for trusting me.

You all are my heart.

Love to all,

P.S. If you don't already have a real estate agent, and you'd like to find one who works like I do, please feel free to call or email me. I can provide you with a referral in which I will stay in touch with you and with the agent to whom I referred you.

If you don't live in Colorado, that's okay. I can still find you an exemplary real estate agent anywhere across the country.

My cell is (970) 210-1161, and my email is CindySellsMore@Gmail.com.

I would love to help you!

Notes

Notes

Notes

Notes

Notes

Notes

Notes

Notes

Notes

Made in the USA
Columbia, SC
13 March 2025